Electricity in the Real World

by Sarah E. Ward

Content Consultant
Peter Barnes
Astrophysicist
University of Florida

CORE
LIBRARY

Published by ABDO Publishing Company, PO Box 398166, Minneapolis, MN 55439. Copyright © 2013 by Abdo Consulting Group, Inc. International copyrights reserved in all countries. No part of this book may be reproduced in any form without written permission from the publisher. The Core Library™ is a trademark and logo of ABDO Publishing Company.

Printed in the United States of America,
North Mankato, Minnesota
112012
012013
♻ THIS BOOK CONTAINS AT LEAST 10% RECYCLED MATERIALS.

Editor: Karen Latchana Kenney
Series Designer: Becky Daum

Cataloging-in-Publication Data
Ward, Sarah E.
 Electricity in the real world / Sarah E. Ward.
   p. cm. -- (Science in the real world)
Includes bibliographical references and index.
ISBN 978-1-61783-738-8
1. Electricity--Juvenile literature.   I. Title.
537--dc21
                                                    2012946827

Photo Credits: Stuart Monk/Shutterstock Images, cover, 1; Sarawut Padungkwan/Shutterstock Images, 4; DK Images, 7, 32; Shutterstock Images, 9, 18, 22, 24, 26, 29, 45; SSPL/Getty Images, 10, 16; Omikron/Getty Images, 13; Photo Researchers/Getty Images, 15; Red Line Editorial, 20, 27; Studio Box/Getty Images, 30; Waterloo Courier, Matthew Putney/AP Images, 34; Vaclav Volrab/Shutterstock Images, 36; Bill Green/The Boston Globe/Getty Images, 40

CONTENTS

CHAPTER ONE

Electricity Is Everywhere

When most people think of electricity, they think about flipping a light switch or plugging in an appliance. But these are just two ways people use electricity. You use it to power many things in your life.

Did you wash your hands or face this morning? Your home's hot water heater probably needs electricity to work. And there's a small amount of

We access electricity by putting a plug in an outlet.

Batteries

We use batteries in many kinds of machines—from laptops to cell phones. A battery creates electricity through a chemical reaction. It also stores energy for later use. Some batteries run out of electricity after a while. They must be thrown out. Other batteries, such as the ones used in cell phones, can be recharged. They last much longer.

electricity in your body. Your body uses it to send messages to and from your brain. Foods such as milk, eggs, and juice stay fresh longer when they're kept cold. Refrigerators run on electricity, and so do toasters and microwaves. Have you taken laundry out from a dryer and found a sock stuck to a towel? That's static electricity. Television remotes and tablet computers have batteries. They use electricity too.

Atoms and Electrons

When describing electricity, you need to know about atoms. Everything in the world is made of atoms. An atom is like a tiny cluster of protons and neutrons inside a larger shell of electrons. Each atom has a

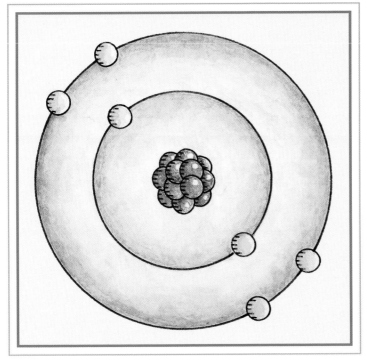

An atom has electrons, *yellow*, in shells around a central nucleus, *green and red.*

nucleus at its center. Protons and neutrons are inside the nucleus. Electrons move around the nucleus in shells.

Around one shell is another shell, and so on. The number of shells depends on the element. Hydrogen has one electron in one shell. Copper has 29 electrons in four shells.

Electricity is possible because of how atoms work. A force such as friction can separate an electron from an atom. Separating electrons from their atoms

Electricity at Home

Different machines use different amounts of electricity. The use is measured in watts. Here are a few machines and the watts needed to power them:

- computer (monitor and printer): 200 watts
- television: 180 watts
- toaster: 1,150 watts
- hair dryer: 1,000 watts

creates positive and negative charges. This is static electricity. It is one form of electricity. Another form of electricity comes in a current along a wire. This form can be made in batteries or power plants. We use this kind of electricity to power machines.

The rate that energy is supplied or used up is the electrical power. A watt is the unit of measure for electrical power.

Different kitchen tools use different amounts of watts to work.

CHAPTER TWO

Discovering Electricity

n 1600 William Gilbert discovered that rubbing certain materials together produced static electricity. In 1745 scientists learned they could store static electricity in a special glass jar, called the Leyden jar.

In the mid-1700s, static electricity was strangely popular. In the mid-1700s, scientists and nonscientists alike were interested in static electricity. Benjamin

Leyden jars were once used to store static electricity.

Franklin was a man with an interest in science. This led him to experiment with static electricity. In 1752 he found that lightning was a type of static electricity.

Luigi Galvani discovered a connection between static electricity and muscle movement in 1786. While working with a machine, a friend touched a dead frog's leg with a knife. A spark came from the machine. The frog's leg moved as a result. Alessandro Volta built on Galvani's work to create a simple battery in 1800. He layered the metals zinc and silver with cardboard soaked in salt water to form the battery.

Putting Electricity to Work

In 1819 Hans Christian Øersted discovered the connection between electricity and magnetism. Øersted found that changing electrical currents made a magnetic field. And he found that changing magnetic fields created an electrical current. Before this time, no one thought that magnetism and electricity were related. It was a brand-new idea.

Allesandro Volta's battery, seen behind him on a table, made electricity.

Choosing Currents

Two kinds of electrical currents are used: alternating current (AC) and direct current (DC). Thomas Edison hired Nikola Tesla to work in his Menlo Park, New Jersey, lab. Tesla began with AC instead of DC. By 1887 he had filed for seven patents. Edison felt strongly that DC was better, and he even spoke against AC. But AC was found to be far more efficient than DC when electricity was sent over long distances.

This discovery led Michael Faraday to create a very simple electric motor in 1821. In 1831 he discovered that a moving magnet could create an electrical current in a coil of wire. He had created the first electromagnet. Faraday's discovery made it clear that electrical power was going to be useful. Scientists and engineers began looking for ways to put electricity to work.

One important use for electricity is lighting. After many tries, Thomas Edison made a long-lasting lightbulb in 1879. Edison opened a power station in 1882 to provide electricity to homes and businesses. This plant generated DC electricity.

English scientist Michael Faraday experimented with electricity and magnets.

Nikola Tesla's invention of AC power made moving electricity over long distances easier.

In 1887 Nikola Tesla invented a transformer. This device makes it easier to send AC electricity over long distances. Throughout the 1900s, the demand for electricity grew as more machines were invented. Power plants created the electricity needed. And power lines delivered that electricity to its many users.

Michael Faraday wrote a letter to German chemist Eilhard Mitscherlich on January 24, 1837. He discussed how the study of electricity and chemistry might be linked:

> *I have been so electrically occupied of late that I feel as if hungry for a little chemistry: but then the conviction crosses my mind that these things hang together under one law & that the more haste we make onwards each in his own path the sooner we shall arrive, and meet each other, at that state of knowledge of natural causes from which all varieties of effects may be understood & enjoyed.*

Source: Michael Faraday. The Correspondence of Michael Faraday, Vol. 2. Ed. Frank A. J. L. James. London: The Institution of Electrical Engineers, 1993. Print. 488.

Consider Your Audience

Read Faraday's letter closely. How could you adapt the letter for a different audience, such as your parents or younger friends? Write a blog post conveying this same information for the new audience. What is the best way to get your point across to this audience?

CHAPTER THREE

Electrical Circuits

In an electrical current, electrons are constantly moving. When an electrical current moves, it can do work, such as turn on a lightbulb. Electrical current moves through a circuit. Current can only flow when the circuit is a closed loop. That means that all the parts of the circuit are connected. When the loop is not complete, the circuit is open. Electricity cannot flow. The device on the circuit that the electricity

A complete circuit allows the lights in your home to be turned on.

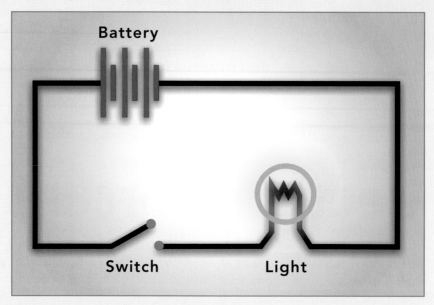

Simple Electrical Circuit

This diagram shows how a simple electrical circuit works to turn on a light. It has a switch, light, battery, and wire. Compare how this information is conveyed visually in the diagram with how it's conveyed in the text. How does the diagram help you understand the text better? How are the text and the diagram different?

operates is called the load. The amount of current is measured in amperes, or amps.

Turning on a light switch closes a circuit. Electricity flows from a connection to the house, through wires in the house, and into wires in the light fixture. Then it flows through a small wire in the lightbulb and back through the fixture through another wire. When you turn the switch off, you open the circuit and the current stops flowing.

In a circuit, voltage is a kind of force that makes electrons flow when a circuit is closed. Voltage is measured in volts.

Conductors and Insulators

There are two important types of materials used with electricity. One type is a conductor. It allows electricity to move from one spot to another. Metals and salt water are examples of conductors. The other material is an insulator. It protects and contains the electricity flow. Rubber and plastic are insulators. The prongs on an electrical plug are metal. The main part of the plug is plastic. It keeps the current away from your hand.

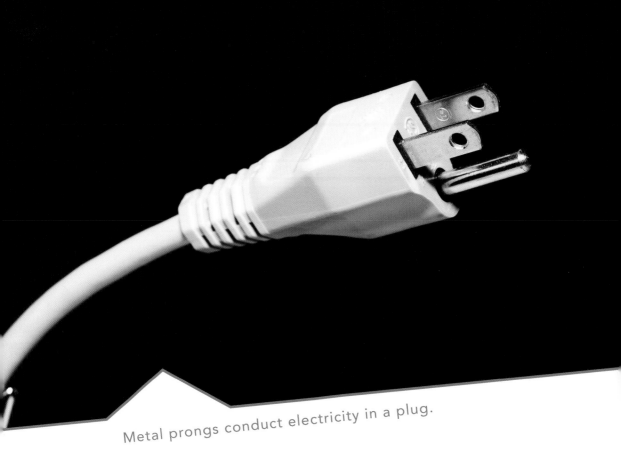

Metal prongs conduct electricity in a plug.

Resistance

When electrons move through a conductor, some of the electrons meet resistance. Anything that increases collisions between electrons and atoms increases resistance. For example, a long copper wire has more resistance than a short one. The electrons have more chances to collide with copper atoms. The resistance takes some of the energy away from the current. Less energy is available to use. The temperature of the wire also affects resistance. At warmer temperatures, the copper atoms move faster. Electrons are more likely to collide with the atoms.

FURTHER EVIDENCE

There is quite a bit of information about electricity in Chapter Three. It covers circuits, conductors, insulators, and resistance. But if you could pick out the main point of the chapter, what would it be? What evidence was given to support that point? Visit the Web site below to learn more about circuits. Choose a quote from the Web site that relates to this chapter. Does this quote support the author's main point? Does it make a new point? Write a few sentences explaining how the quote you found relates to this chapter.

How Do Electric Circuits Work?

www.kids.discovery.com/tell-me/curiosity-corner/science/how-do-electric-circuits-work

CHAPTER FOUR

Making and Moving Electricity

Power is delivered to many places through electric current. But first energy must be changed into electricity. A generator is a machine that makes electricity. The energy it uses can come from a fuel, the wind, the sun, or nuclear reactions.

Solar panels can turn sun energy into electricity.

A transformer helps electricity move from power stations to places where it can be used.

Electromagnetism

In an electromagnet generator, a coil of wire moves around a magnet. A power source is needed to get the coil of wire to move. In the United States, coal or natural gas is the power source for approximately two-thirds of the country's electrical generators. The fuel is burned to heat water. The water turns into steam. The steam pushes against blades of a turbine.

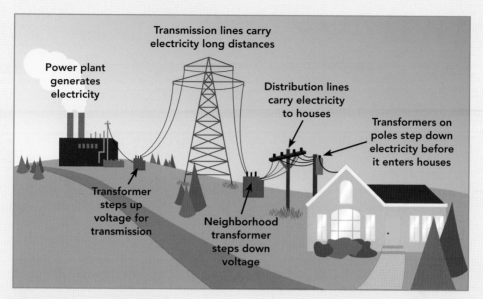

The Electricity Path

This diagram shows how electricity travels from a power plant to a person's home. Compare how this information is conveyed visually in the diagram with how it's conveyed in the text. How are the text and the diagram similar? How are they different?

The energy from the turbine moves the coil around the magnet. This generates an electrical current.

Stepping Up and Stepping Down

Once electricity is produced at a power plant, it has to get to customers. That means electricity must travel long distances. The voltage produced at a power plant is much, much larger than what homes and businesses need. Transformers change the voltage so people can use it.

Inside a transformer are two coils of wire close to a magnet. Electrical current enters the transformer through one coil and leaves through the other. This changes the voltage. Step-down transformers take high-voltage current and change it to a lower voltage. Step-up transformers take low voltage and change it to a higher voltage.

Thick wire cables carry the current away from the step-up transformer to distribution centers. At the distribution centers, the current goes through step-down transformers. The electricity is changed to a level needed for

Power Line Workers

Working on high-voltage power lines can be very dangerous. Workers risk death if electrical current goes through their bodies. Workers wear special gloves. These two-layer gloves have rubber on the inside and leather on the outside. The rubber is a good insulator. The leather protects the rubber from tearing.

Electricity meters measure electricity usage.

customers in the area. Near homes the current is stepped down again in transformers on utility poles.

Meters and Fuse Boxes

As the electricity enters a home or business, it goes through a meter. The meter measures the amount of electricity that a location uses. Then the electricity heads to the fuse box. This is a safety device. It stops the flow of electricity in the event of an electrical problem. Finally the current goes through the wiring in the walls and ceiling to all the devices that use it. Then it is ready when the customer needs it.

CHAPTER FIVE

Electricity in Humans

Electricity powers machines, but it also powers the human body. Too much electricity passing through a human body is harmful. It can even cause death. But people couldn't live without a little electricity flowing in their bodies.

The systems in a human body communicate through electrical signals. They let a person respond quickly to danger. If a woman touches something

Electrical signals tell us when something is too hot to touch.

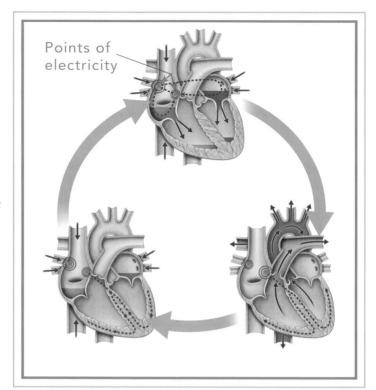

Points of electricity

Electricity makes the heart pump blood to the rest of the body.

hot, an electrical signal moves from her fingers to the reflex system in her spine. The reflex system sends a message to the muscles in her hand. She pulls her hand away from the heat.

In a human body, electrons flow from one cell to another. When a cell is at rest, it has a small negative charge. The area just outside the cell has a small positive charge. This difference in charges allows electrical signals to move from cell to cell.

Electrical Charge in the Heart

Electrical signals in the human heart make it pump blood. The electrical signal starts when the smaller chambers at the top of the heart fill with blood. The signal moves down through these chambers causing them to contract. The signal continues to the base of the heart. It then causes the lower chambers to contract. The contractions push blood out of the heart.

An electrocardiograph is a machine that can record the heart's electrical signals. Healthcare workers look at the machine's results to see if the heart is working normally.

Animal Electricity

Small electrical signals flow through animals too. Electric eels have cells in their body that store electricity. The eels use small electrical charges to locate prey. To capture prey, the eel can use a voltage that's five times stronger than the voltage in a home outlet. Sharks have special sense organs that detect electricity. This helps them find nearby prey.

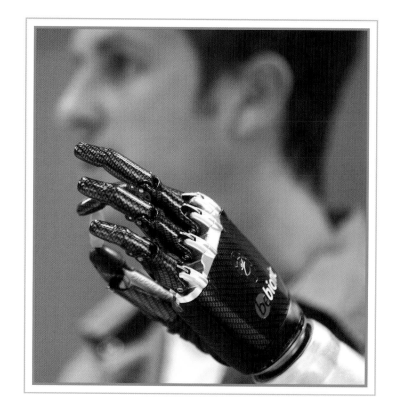

A Bebionic 3 artificial hand features electric fingers.

Touch Screens

Tablet computers, some cell phones, and many other electronic devices have touch screens. These screens use electricity to work. One kind of touch screen works because of the electrical current in a bare hand. On the inside of the screen is a fine grid of electrical conductors. Touching a point on the grid completes a circuit. The location of the circuit tells the computer what the user touched.

Artificial Limbs

An artificial limb is used when part of an arm or leg is missing. Straps attach artificial limbs to the body.

Many artificial limbs use electrical signals from the muscles where the limb is connected. These small electrical signals operate the artificial limb. A plastic skin-like covering helps the limb look real too.

EXPLORE ONLINE

The focus in Chapter Five was the electricity found in humans. It also touched upon how electricity works in the heart. The Web site below focuses on the heart's electrical system. As you know, every source is different. How is the information given in the Web site different from the information in this chapter? What information is the same? How do the two sources present information differently? What can you learn from this Web site?

Your Heart's Electrical System
www.uofmchildrenshospital.org/healthlibrary/Article/82063

CHAPTER SIX

The Future of Electricity

Most US homes didn't have electricity until the early 1900s. What was everyday life like before then? It was very dark at night. Indoor lights included candles, kerosene lamps, and a few natural gas fixtures. It was cold in the winter. Heat came from fireplaces and stoves fueled by coal or wood. US electricity use has changed a lot since then.

Wind turbines may become a more common way to make electricity in the future.

Stealth Technology

Electricity can be used to make planes seem invisible. This is part of stealth technology. People find and track planes using radar signals. Radar sends out electric and magnetic waves to find objects. When the waves reflect off an object, the radar operator can locate the object. Electricity from a plane with stealth technology jams radar signals. Without the return signals, radars cannot see planes with this technology.

How will electricity's use change in the next 100 years?

Electricity's Usefulness

Using electricity in health care has changed many types of treatments. Electricity will continue to play an important role in health care. Researchers are exploring more advanced sensors on artificial limbs. Instead of placing sensors on the artificial limb, researchers are putting sensors on muscles inside the body. They want to know if electrical signals from a person's brain can activate the sensors to use the artificial limb.

Other researchers are exploring how electricity can help relieve serious and long-lasting pain.

Electrical signals that the body sends to the brain can cause people to feel pain. Scientists want to find out if interrupting these electrical signals can stop pain.

Challenges of Generating Electricity

There are challenges to generating electricity. Most power plants in the world use fossil fuels to generate electricity. But fossil fuels are limited. They also produce pollution. Using nuclear energy leads to less pollution. But it leaves leftover materials, or nuclear waste. This waste is dangerous and must be stored securely for a long time—in some cases for thousands of years. What will power plants use for fuel in the future?

Another challenge of generating electricity is that key parts of the power grid are aging. The power grid is the system used to get power from power plants to places where it can be used. Power transformers are built to last between 40 and 50 years. In 2012 their average age was 42 years. That means that

Workers at a power control center track power outages.

transformers may begin failing in the next decade. Owners and managers of power plants need up-to-date plans for handling equipment problems. Workers on power lines and at distribution centers need to recognize and respond to these problems quickly. Otherwise power outages can spread through the power grid.

Electricity has become an important part of daily life. It powers many machines that make work and life easier for us in different ways. Electricity will continue to be a useful tool into the future.

In a 2010 speech, computer programmer and businessman Bill Gates spoke about energy, electricity, and pollution. He said:

> *Now, the price of energy has come down over time. Really advanced civilization is based on advances in energy. . . . even in the 1900s we've seen a very rapid decline in the price of electricity, and that's why we have refrigerators, air-conditioning, we can make modern materials and do so many things. And so, we're in a wonderful situation with electricity in the rich world. But, as we make it cheaper — and let's go for making it twice as cheap — we need to meet a new constraint, and that constraint has to do with [carbon dioxide].*
>
> *Source: Bill Gates. "Bill Gates on Energy: Innovating to Zero!" TED. TED Conferences, February 2010. Web. Accessed October 24, 2012.*

What's the Big Idea?

Read Gates's speech carefully. What is his main idea? Explain how the main idea is supported by details. Name two or three of those supporting details.

IMPORTANT DATES

1600
William Gilbert discovers that rubbing certain materials together produces static electricity.

1745
Scientists learn they can store static electricity in a Leyden jar.

1786
Luigi Galvani discovers a connection between static electricity and muscle movement.

1800
Alessandro Volta uses metals and salt water to create the first battery.

1819
Hans Christian Øersted discovers the connection between electricity and magnetism.

1831
Michael Faraday uses a magnet to create an electrical current.

1879
Thomas Edison makes a long-lasting lightbulb.

1882
To provide power to customers, Thomas Edison opens a power station.

1887
Nikola Tesla develops the transformer.

1900s
Electricity begins to be used in US homes in the early part of the century.

2012
The average age of US power transformers is 42 years old.

OTHER WAYS YOU CAN FIND ELECTRICITY IN THE REAL WORLD

Thomas Edison National Historic Park

Thomas Edison's former laboratory and home is in West Orange, New Jersey. The complex has been preserved and is now a national park. Visitors can tour Edison's laboratory and home, plus other exhibit spaces. To learn more, visit the park's Web site: www.nps.gov/edis/index.htm

Hybrid and Electric Cars

The first electric cars were invented almost 100 years ago. But they weren't practical because the batteries could not be recharged. Hybrid cars, which most commonly have gasoline and electric motors, are more practical.

The gasoline motor can recharge the batteries that run the electric motor. When the driver lightly presses on the brakes, the car's wheels connect to an electrical generator and the generator recharges the batteries.

Wind Turbines

For thousands of years, people have used windmills to provide power. They have used it to grind grain and pump water. The windmills of the past have become the huge wind turbines of the present. Wind turbines take the power of the wind and use it to generate electricity. These towering structures may be as tall as 20-story buildings. Their blades may be as long as 200 feet (61 m).

Say What?

Studying about electricity can mean learning a lot of new vocabulary. Find five words in this book you've never seen or heard before. Use a dictionary to find out what they mean. Then write the meanings in your own words, and use each word in a new sentence.

Tell the Tale

This book discusses how Allesandro Volta created a battery. Write 200 words that tell the true story of the history of our understanding of batteries. Be sure to set the scene by describing Volta's materials. Develop a sequence by including Luigi Galvani's earlier observations. Offer a conclusion about if and how Volta's batteries might be used.

Why Do I Care?

This book explains how electricity is used every day. List two or three ways that you use electricity in your life. Imagine that you are unable to use electricity for one day. How do you think it would affect you?

You Are There

Imagine you are Michael Faraday in 1831. You have just discovered that moving a magnet inside a coil of wire makes an electrical current flow in the wire. What questions do you have? How do you change your experiments to answer these questions? Write 300 words about the experiments that help you find the answers.

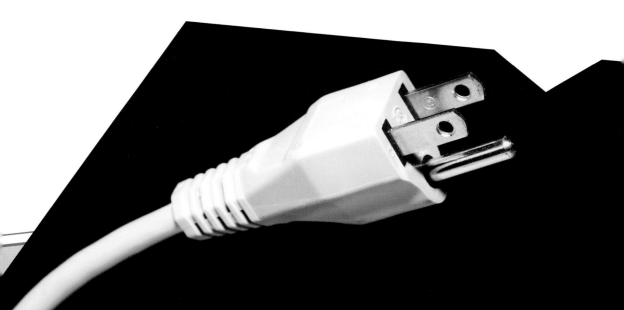

GLOSSARY

ampere
the unit of measure of current

circuit
a closed loop through which electricity can flow

conductor
a material in which electrons can move easily

electromagnet
a coil of wire through which an electrical current passes, creating a magnetic field

insulator
a material that stops the flow of electrons

resistance
the friction that moving electrons encounter

static electricity
a nonmoving electrical charge sometimes created by friction

transformer
a device that increases or decreases the voltage of electrical current

turbine
a machine in which power is made by a wheel that turns from the force of water or other liquid, steam, gas, air

voltage
the force on electrons that causes them to move through a closed circuit

watt
the unit of measure of electrical power

LEARN MORE

Books

Berne, Emma Carlson. *Shocking!: Electricity*.
New York: PowerKids Press, 2013.

Deane-Pratt, Ade. *Electrical Gadgets*. New York:
PowerKids Press, 2012.

Parker, Steve. *Electricity*. New York:
DK Publishing, 2013.

Web Links

To learn more about electricity, visit ABDO Publishing
Company online at **www.abdopublishing.com**.
Web sites about electricity are featured on our Book
Links page. These links are routinely monitored and
updated to provide the most current information
available.

Visit **www.mycorelibrary.com** for free additional tools
for teachers and students.

INDEX

ABOUT THE AUTHOR

Sarah E. Ward's interest in writing began in the sixth grade, when her teacher complimented her short stories. She has worked as a day care teacher, college instructor, and textbook editor. Ward lives in Evanston, Illinois, with her three cats, Keiko, Twix, and Val.